# Daydream Doodles

First edition for the United States
and Canada published in 2015
by Barron's Educational Series, Inc.

Published in 2015 by
Carlton Books Limited
20 Mortimer Street,
London W1T 3JW

Author: Caroline Rowlands
Art Editor: Emily Clarke
Executive Editor: Anna Brett
Production: Marion Storz



*All inquiries should be addressed to:*
Barron's Educational Series, Inc.
250 Wireless Boulevard
Hauppauge, NY 11788
www.barronseduc.com

ISBN: 978-1-4380-0641-3

Date of Manufacture: December 2014
Manufactured by: Leo Paper Group
Printed in Heshan, China
9 8 7 6 5 4 3 2 1

Doodle some purrrrfect kittens in the shapes below.

Take one sharp pencil...

...and oodles of doodles of sprinkles and sweets...

...to create some tasty toppings, for these cupcake treats!

Give the cupcake cases some dotty spotty patterns.

LAZY DAYS IN THE SUN ARE SO MUCH FUN!

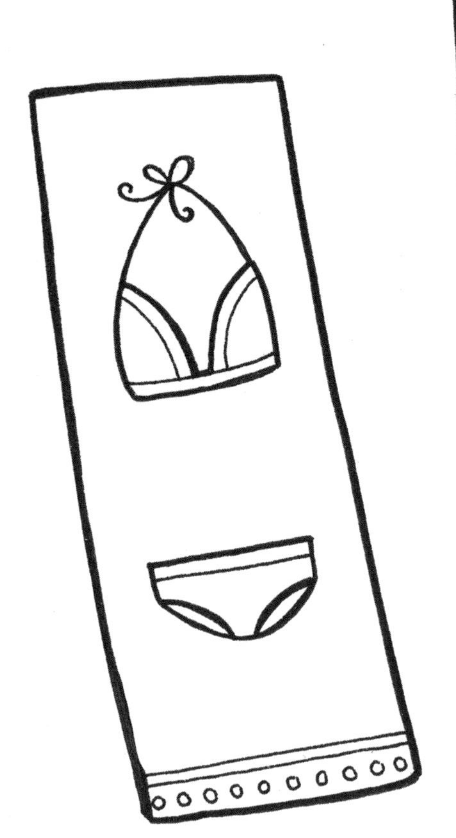

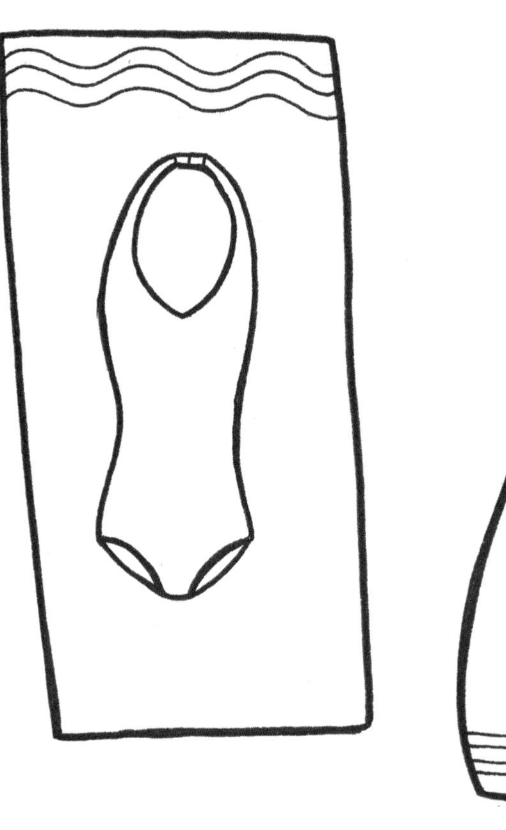

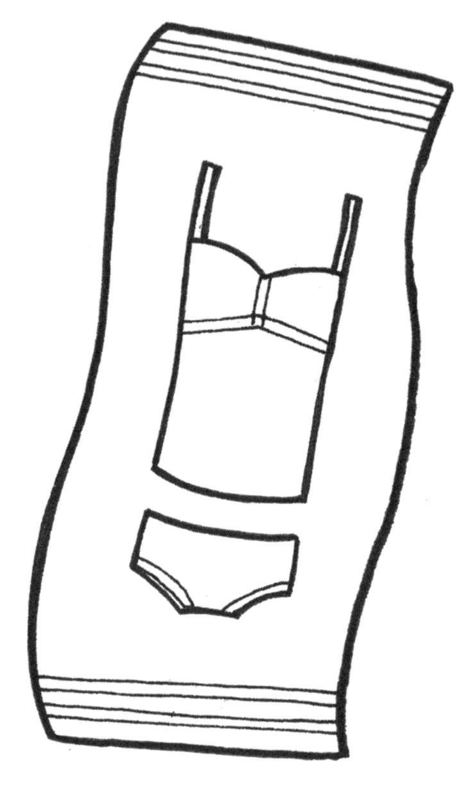

DOODLE A BRIGHT, BOLD DESIGN ON THESE BEACH TOWELS...

...CHILL OUT AND CREATE SOME COOL PATTERNS FOR THESE SWIMSUITS AND BIKINIS.

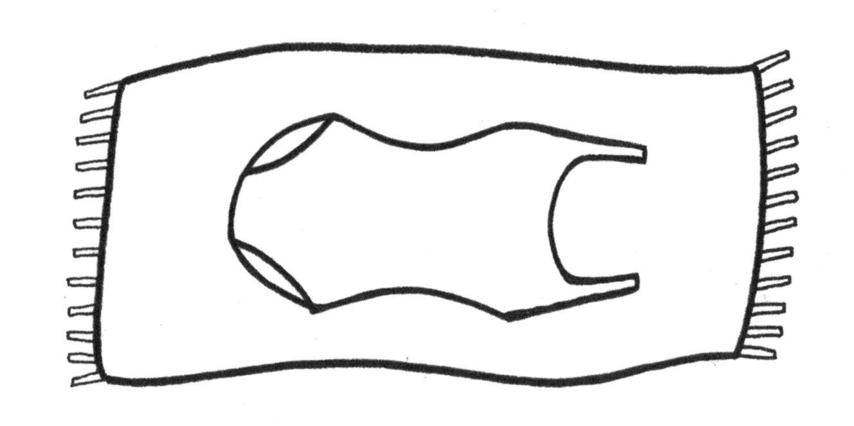

Can you create a doodle ladder?
Start with one doodle, and turn it into something else by the time you reach the top of the ladder.
Start here!

What can you see in the clouds?

WHO IS BOOGYING AWAY ON THE DANCE FLOOR?

The butterfly house has some new arrivals... draw patterns on their beautiful wings.

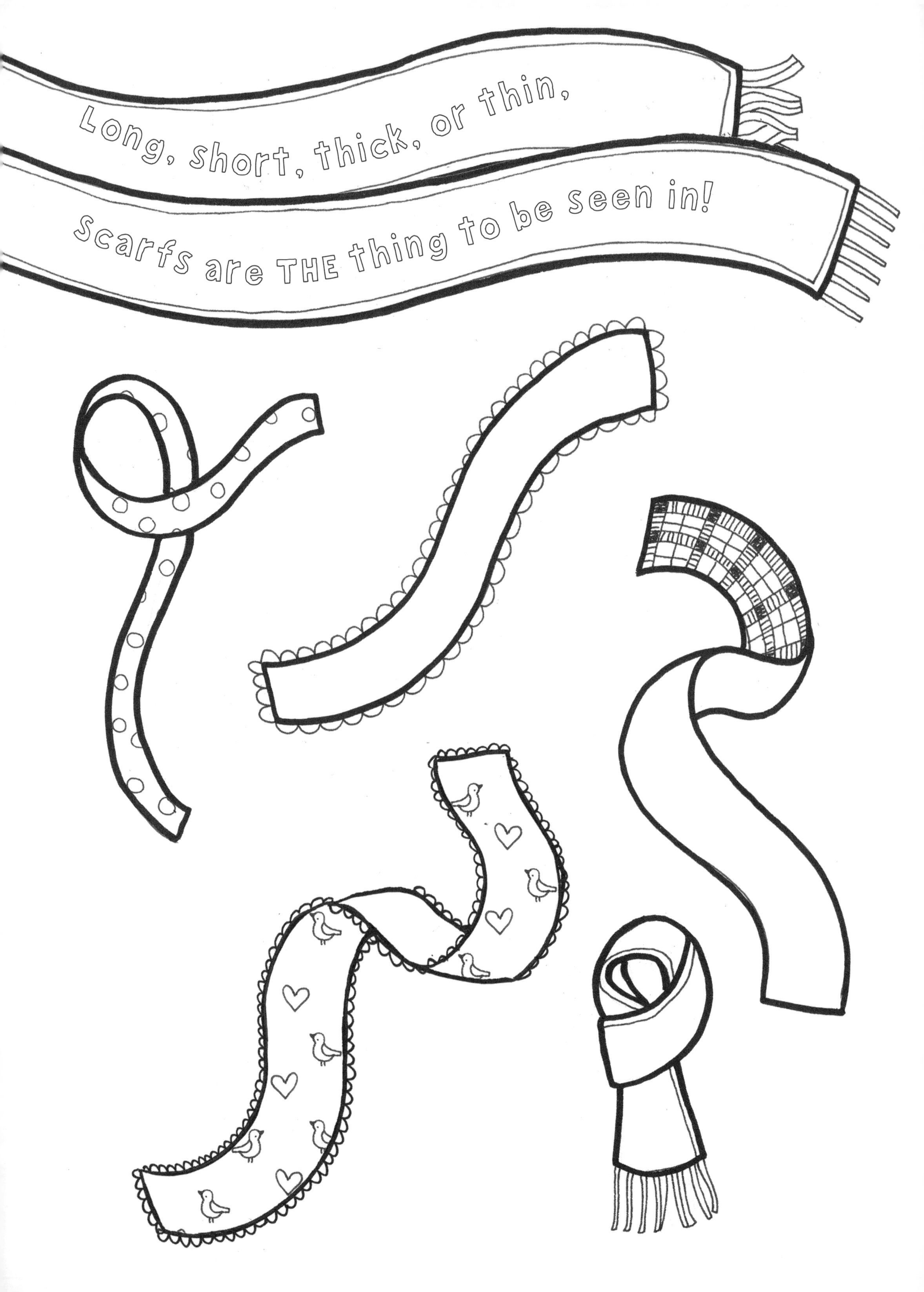
Long, short, thick, or thin,
Scarfs are THE thing to be seen in!

pashmina...
...silk
wool...
...linen

Get growing! Doodle some beautiful blooms around this garden pond...

...then turn
the book
upside down
to doodle
in their
reflection.

WHAT GOES UP....
....MUST COME DOWN!

Make a BIG SPLASH in these puddles with some funny doodles.

Spring has sprung! Turn this book around and help the tree to grow...

Doodle some more roots and bugs deep, deep down in the soil.

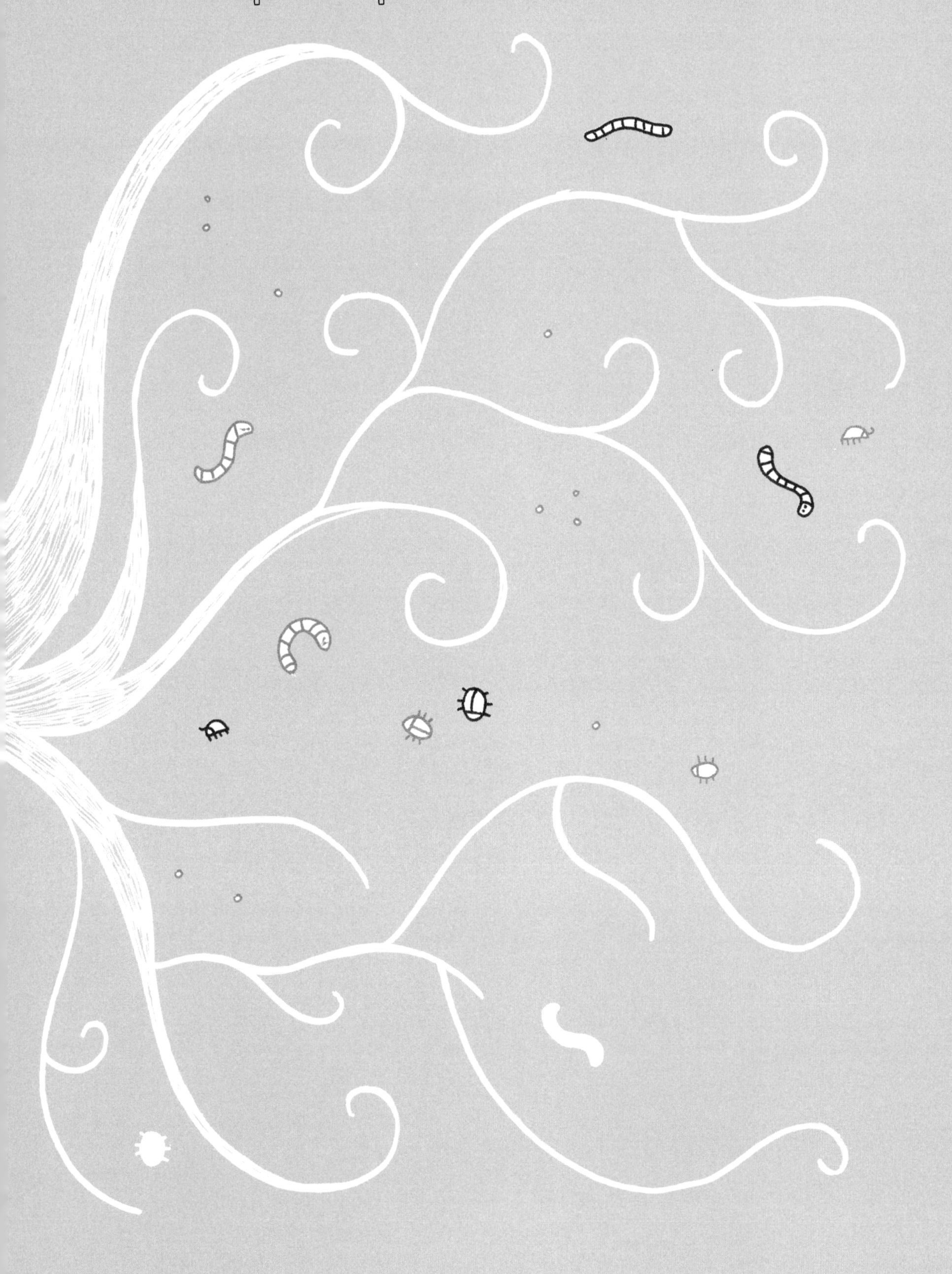

Star light, star bright,
the first star I see tonight.
I wish I may, I wish I might,
Have the wish I wish tonight!

Add some swooshing lines to create a shooting star.

How many heart doodles can you squeeze into this heart?

CLUTCH, SHOULDER, TOTE,
BACKPACK, BOWLING, HOBO,
MESSENGER, SATCHEL...

...DESIGN **YOUR** PERFECT
BAG HERE!

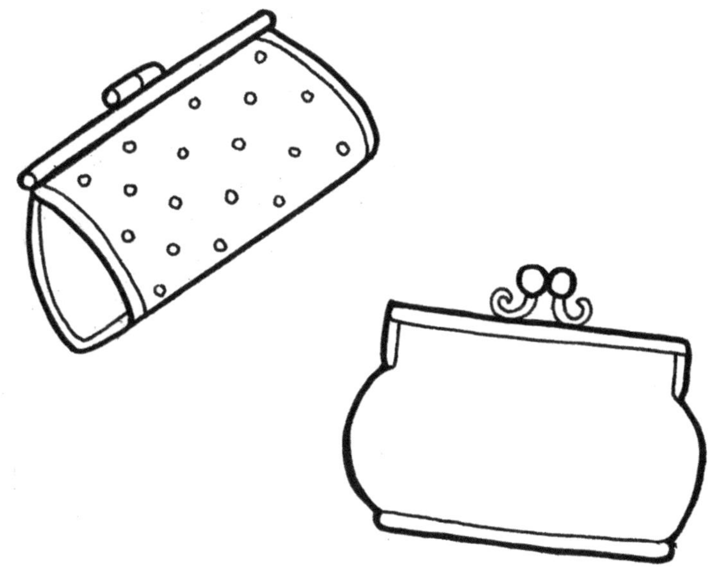

# WHAT'S INSIDE YOUR BAG?

EMPTY OUT YOUR SCHOOLBAG OR HANDBAG AND DRAW EVERYTHING THAT WAS IN IT.

Create the best ice cream in the world EVER!

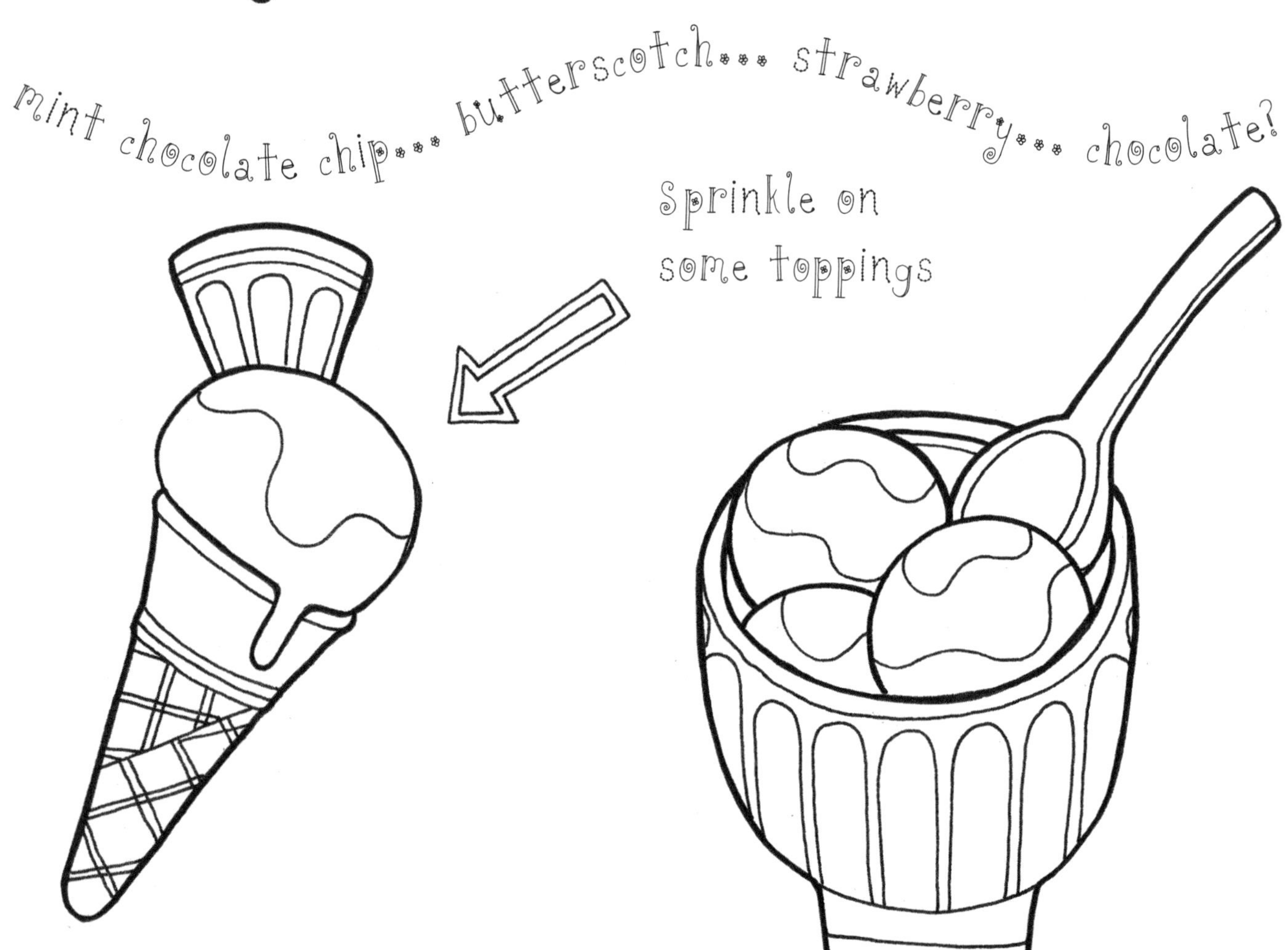

Keep doodling strawberries till you fill up the basket.

# A ONE WAY TICKET TO WHERE?

No. 1

TICKET

No. 2

ONE WAY TICKET

Where do you want to go?
N
W
E
S
Doodle some vacation snapshots.
!!?

BUZZZZZZZZZZZZZZ..........What are these bees flying toward?

Crown your QUEEN BEE with a sparkly  !

BRING ON THE BLING AND CREATE A TIARA FIT FOR A PRINCESS.

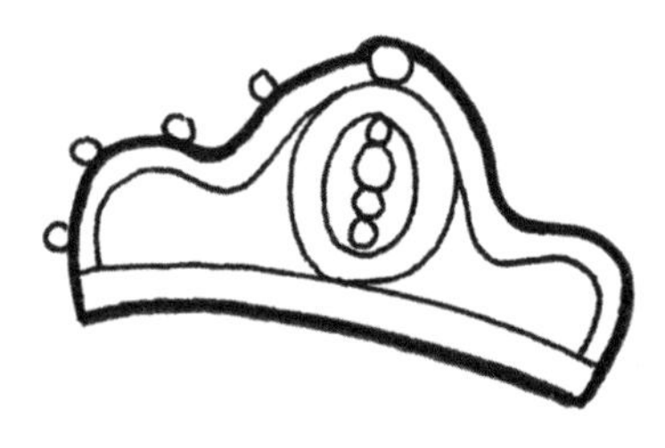

Turn a lickety-lip lollipop into something totally different.

Fill in the frames with
pictures of your family and friends.

Perform your dream dive off the top board!

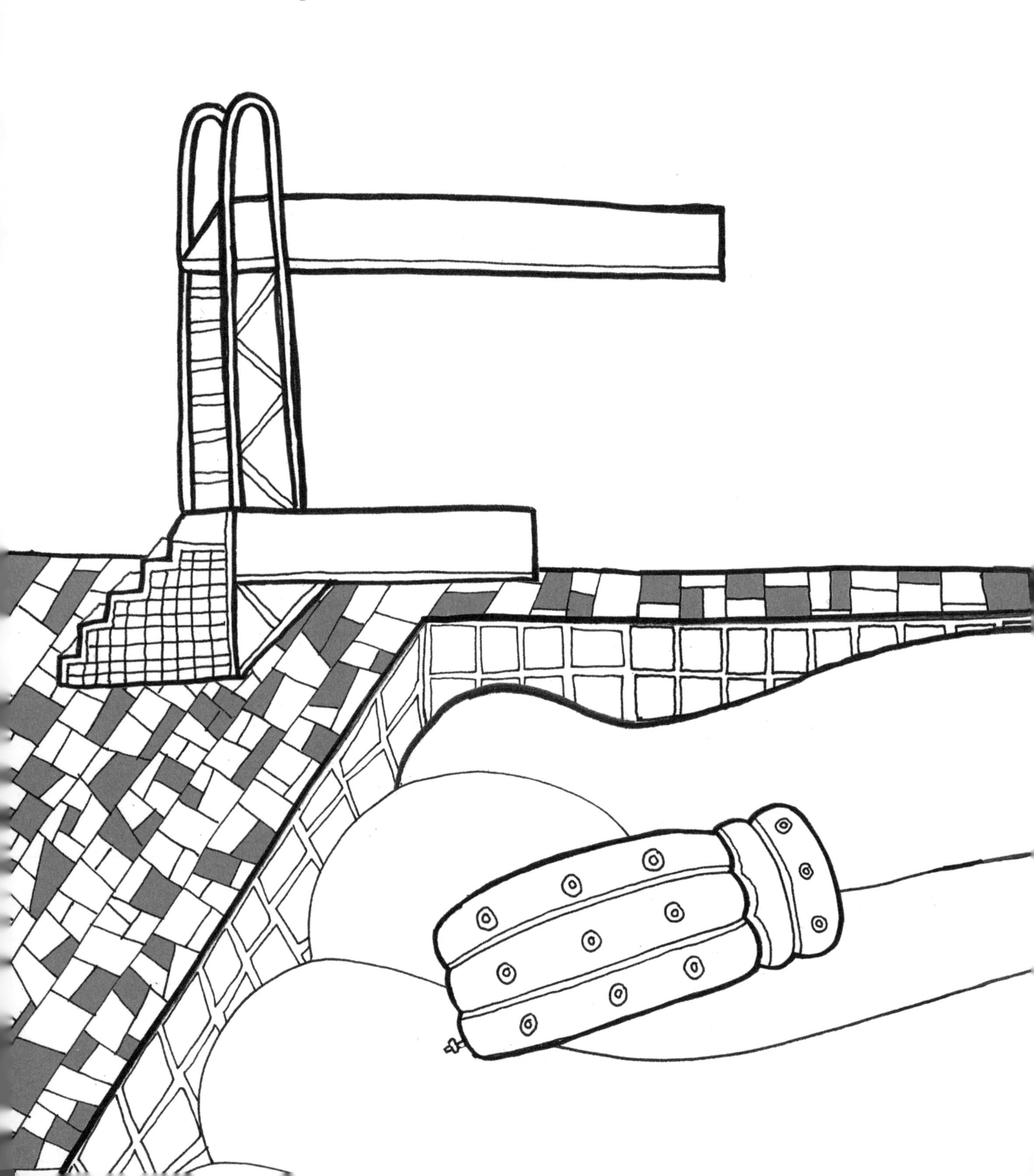

Fill up this pool with happy, splashy swimmers.

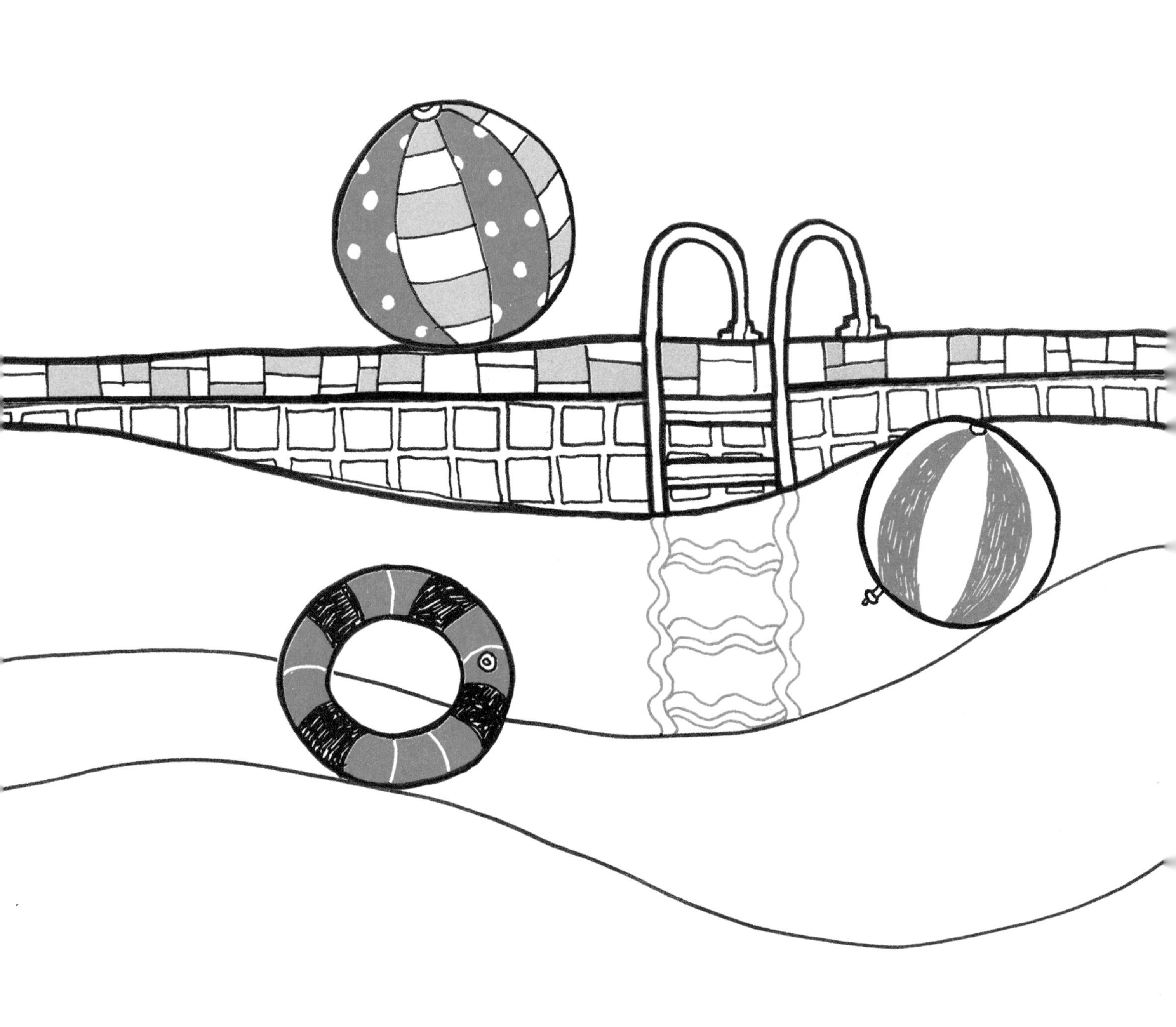

LOOK OUT OF THE NEAREST WINDOW AND DOODLE WHAT YOU CAN SEE.

TICK
TOCK
12
What do you do at 12 o'clock?
Instead of numbers, doodle what you do at each hour on the clock.

Draw a cute, white rabbit in three easy steps.

1. Begin with an egg shape.

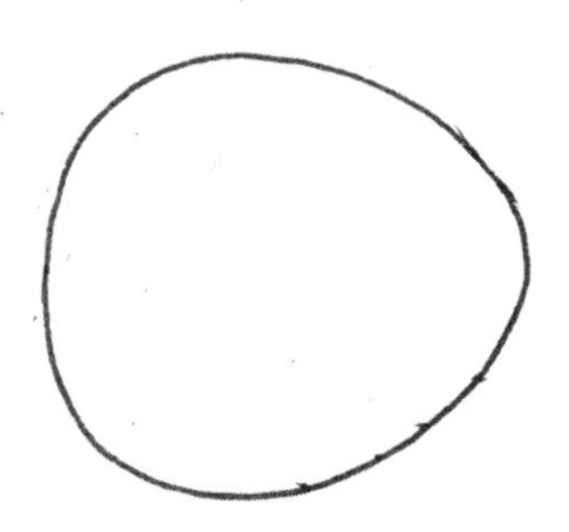

2. Add two more egg shapes, one big, one small.

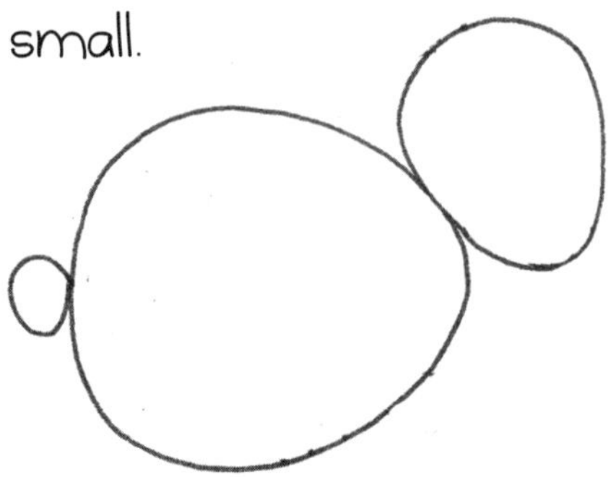

3. Draw in the legs, ears, and an eye.

Doodle your own rabbit here!

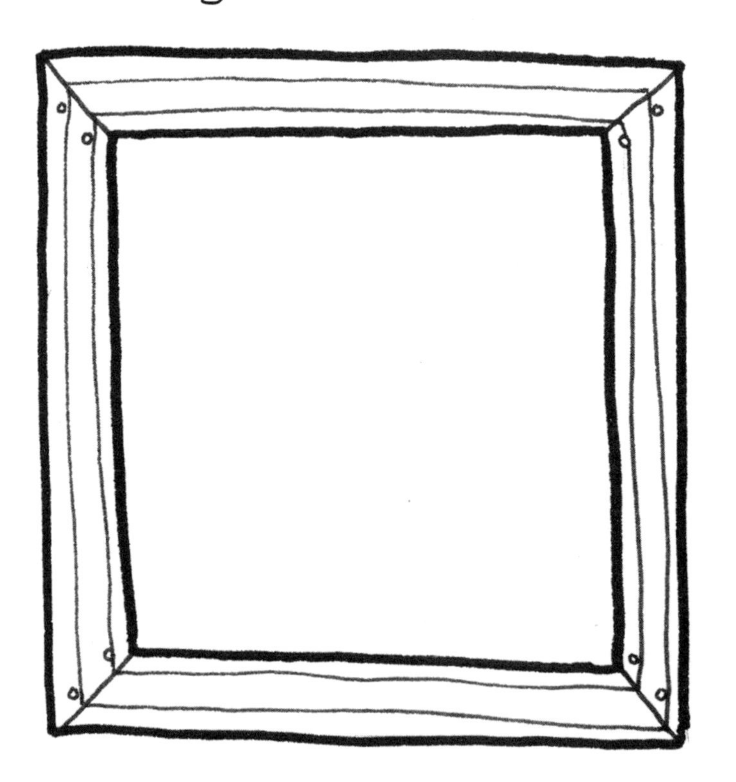

Fill up the holes with some rabbit doodles.
Finish the paw prints.

STARGAZING IN
THE NIGHT SKY...
...WHAT CAN
YOU SEE?

IS THERE ANYONE OUT THERE?

Give this pony a swooshy tail.
Add a cute pattern to this pony's hat.

Doodle a horn to
transform this pony
into a magical unicorn.

# which way up?

create some doodles that look the same, whichever way you look at them.

This way up

Now try this way up

No this way up

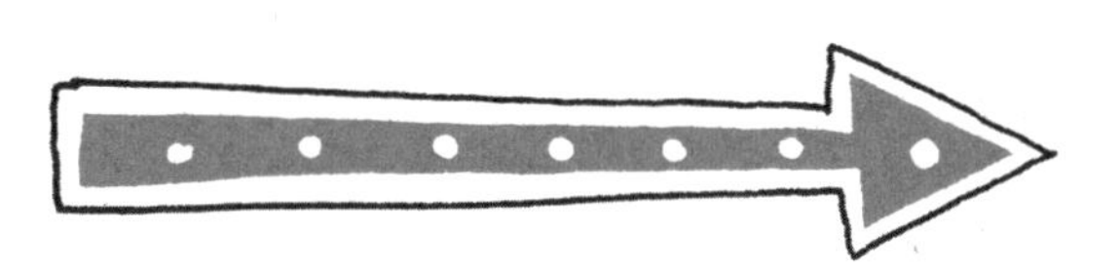

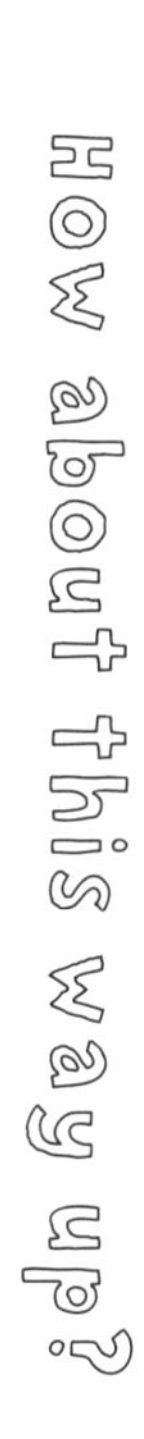


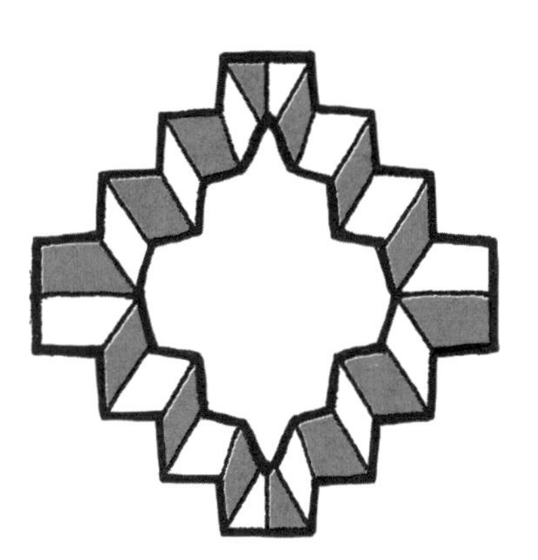

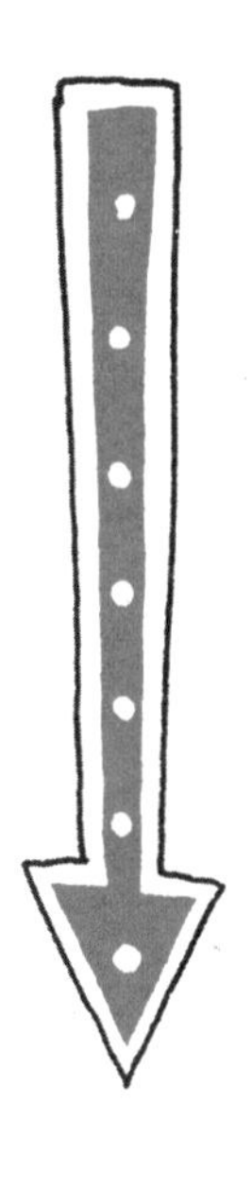

What are mermaids up to
way down
in the deep blue sea?

DO YOUR DOODLES HAVE WHAT
IT TAKES TO BE IN THE
SPOTLIGHT?

Dim the lights by shading in the page black...

...except for this part.

It's showtime! What would you do in the spotlight?

Design some stylish shades for the sunglasses shop.

DOODLE SOME BIRDIES
ON THE WIRES.

Can you doodle a picture that looks like one thing...

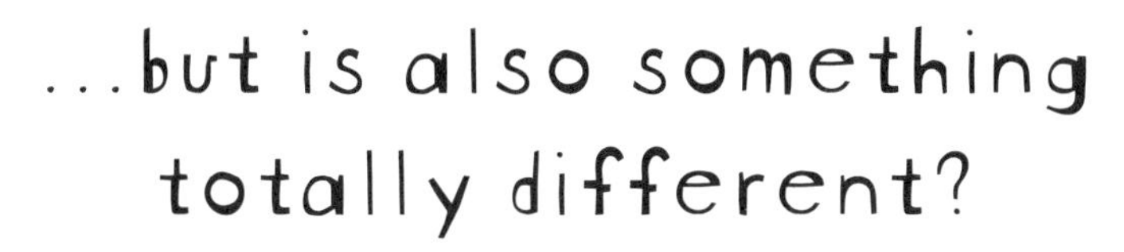

Did you know a hat designer is called a milliner?
Dream up a hat design for this girl to wear.
Sun hat
Cap
Bobble hat
Top hat
Felt hat
Bowler
Fedora
Beret
Boater

Use doodles to create your own comic strip story.

A MAGIC CARPET?

A FLOATING PICNIC RUG?

TURN THIS BLANKET INTO A DOODLE ADVENTURE...

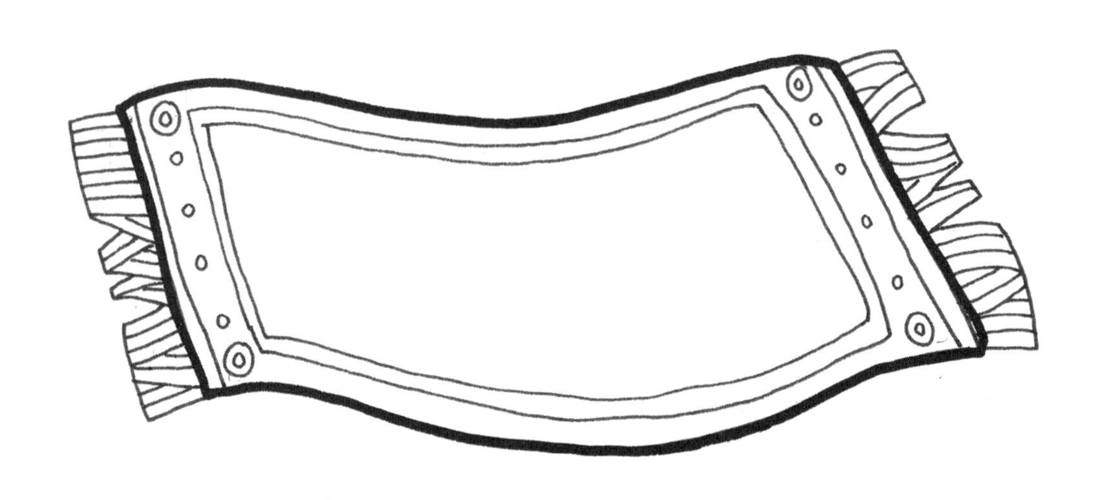

Turn the string from this kite into another doodle...
...then another doodle...
...then another doodle...

This ladybug is one bored insect. Dream up some exciting doodle bugs to entertain her!

Who lives under these
toadstools at the bottom
of the garden?

Doodle your dream home...

HOME SWEET HOME!

SUGAR AND SPICE...
AND ALL THINGS NICE!
HOW DO YOU THINK SWEETS
GET MADE?

# Doodle a BIG elephant in four easy steps.

1. Draw two circles.

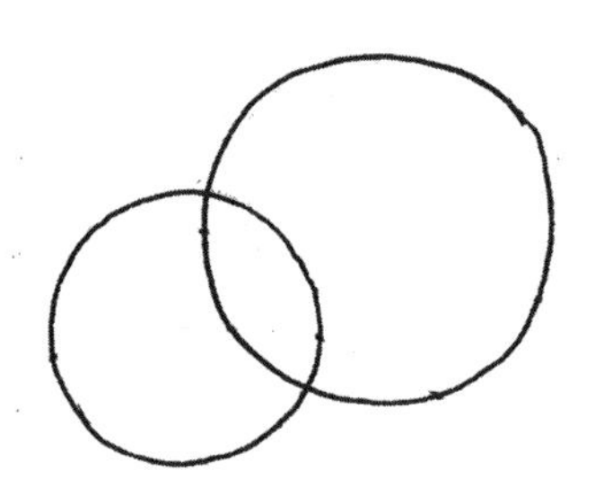

2. Add a large oval underneath them.

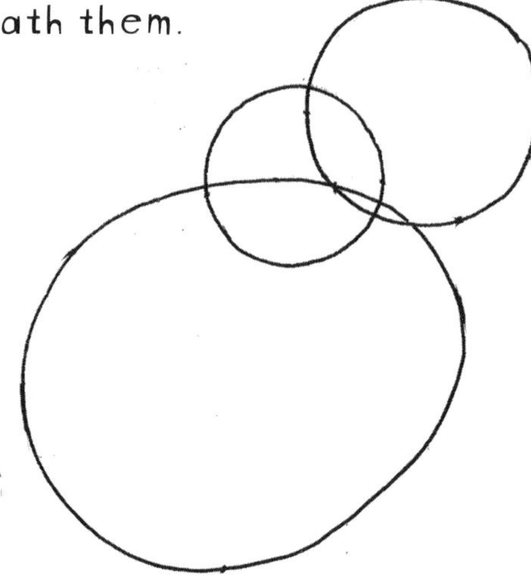

3. Draw a trunk and four legs, and join up the oval and circle to create a mouth.

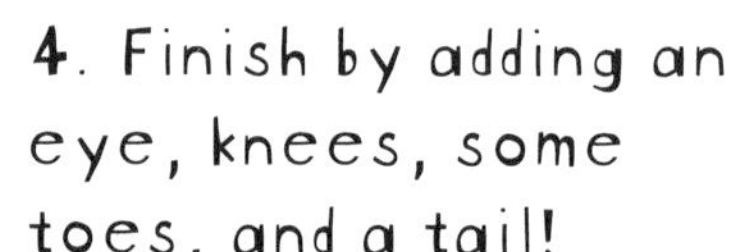

4. Finish by adding an eye, knees, some toes, and a tail!

Where is your elephant?
Doodle a scene behind it.

# Draw a tiny mouse in three simple steps.

1. Start with a line with a swirly tail underneath.

2. Add an arched line for the mouse's body.

3. Finish with an eye, nose, two little ears, and two little paws.

Take a wander in the woods... who is hiding behind the trees?

Draw some tasty fruit growing on these trees!

Doodle in some ingredients to create your favorite dish of the day!

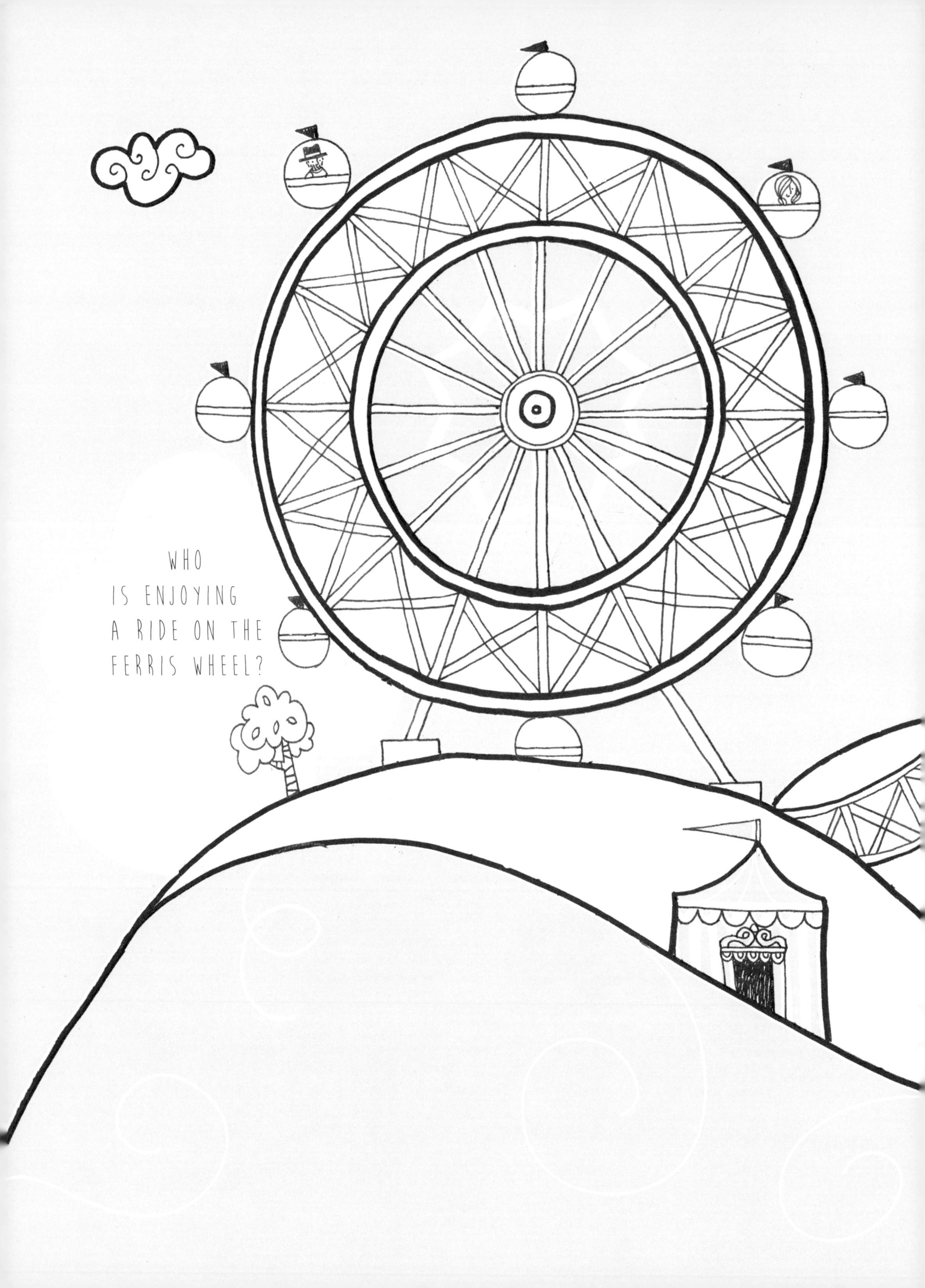
WHO
IS ENJOYING
A RIDE ON THE
FERRIS WHEEL?

JOIN THE
TRACKS AND
FILL IN THE
FACE!

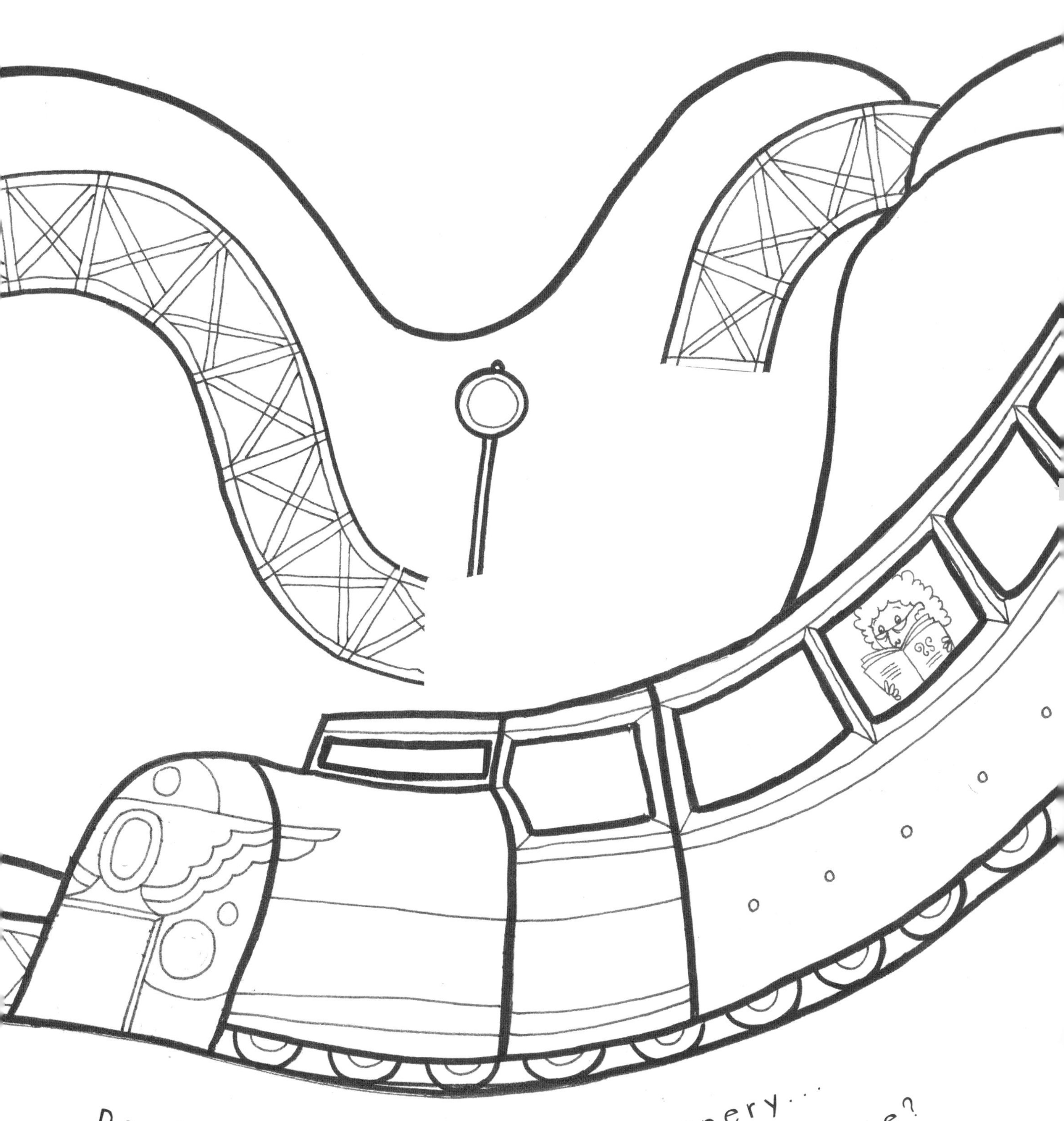

Doodle in some spectacular scenery...

...is there a station along the route?

Look at the sparkling shoes rolling off the production line at Sylvie's Shoe Emporium!

What's at
the end
of the
rainbow?

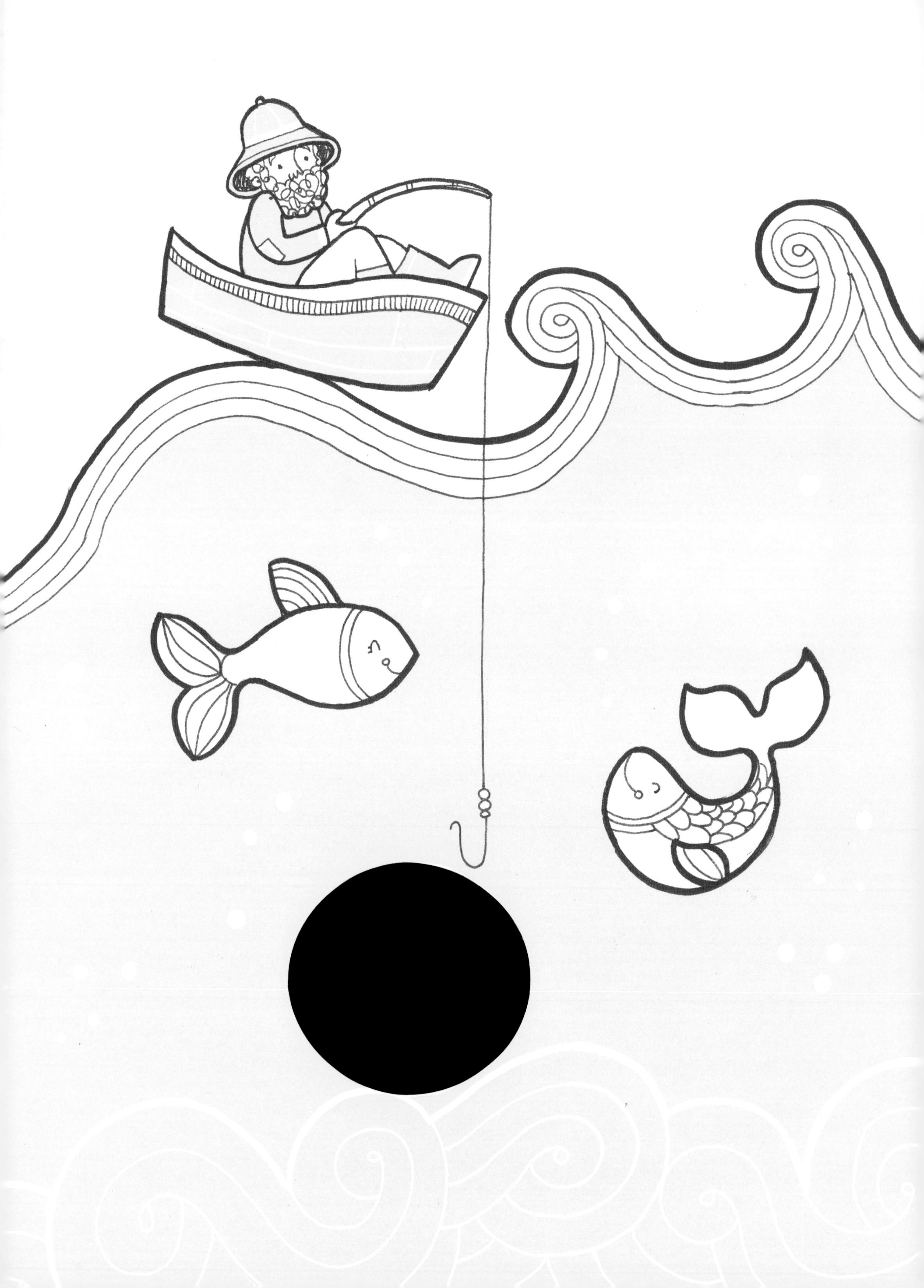

There's so much to see under the sea!

Help the busy hairdresser give this customer some lovely locks.

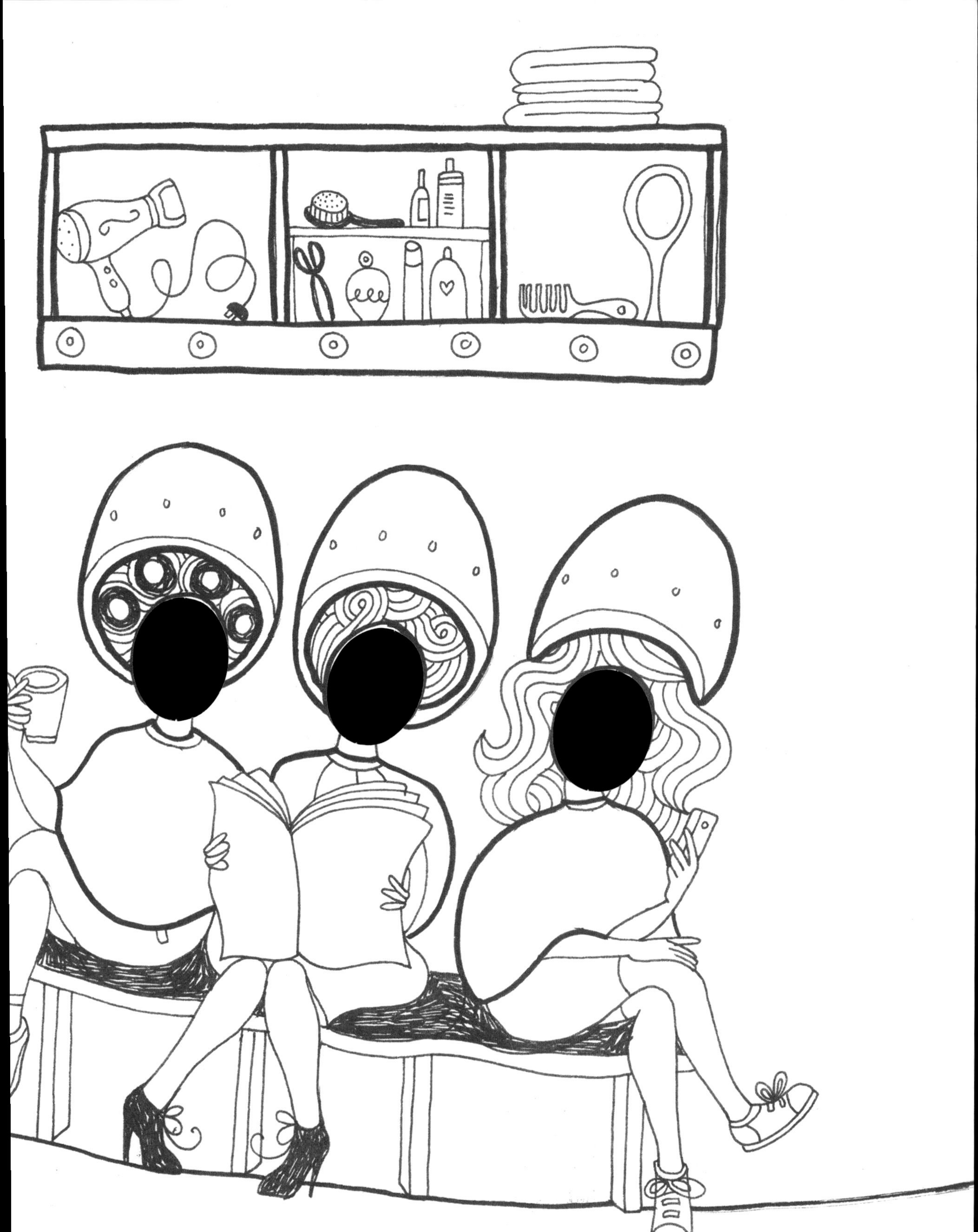

What are these ladies gossiping about?

DOODLE YOUR FAVORITE MOVIE ON THE BIG SCREEN.

What's
coming down the
waterfall?

Turn each letter into something weird and wonderful!

# What's inside?

Add some patterns to these Russian dolls.

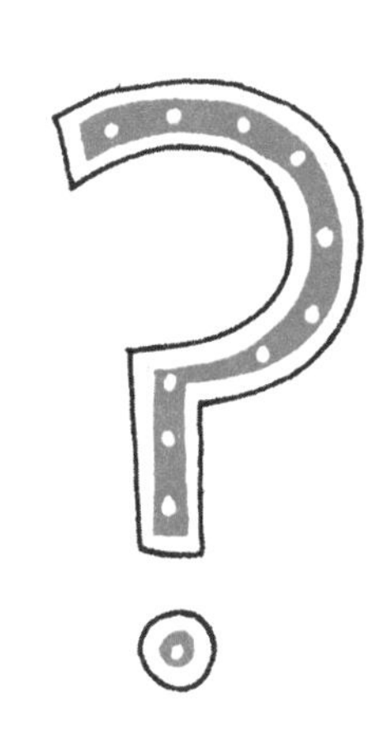

Draw your own dolls... why not try something different!

Late at night, when no one is watching...
...owls get up to all sorts of mischief.

woof woof! grrrrrrrrrowl!

BARK!

Finish off these doggy doodles.

# S.O.S!

Doodle some boats and a castaway on the desert island.

Once upon a time...

...a beautiful princess doodled a castle!

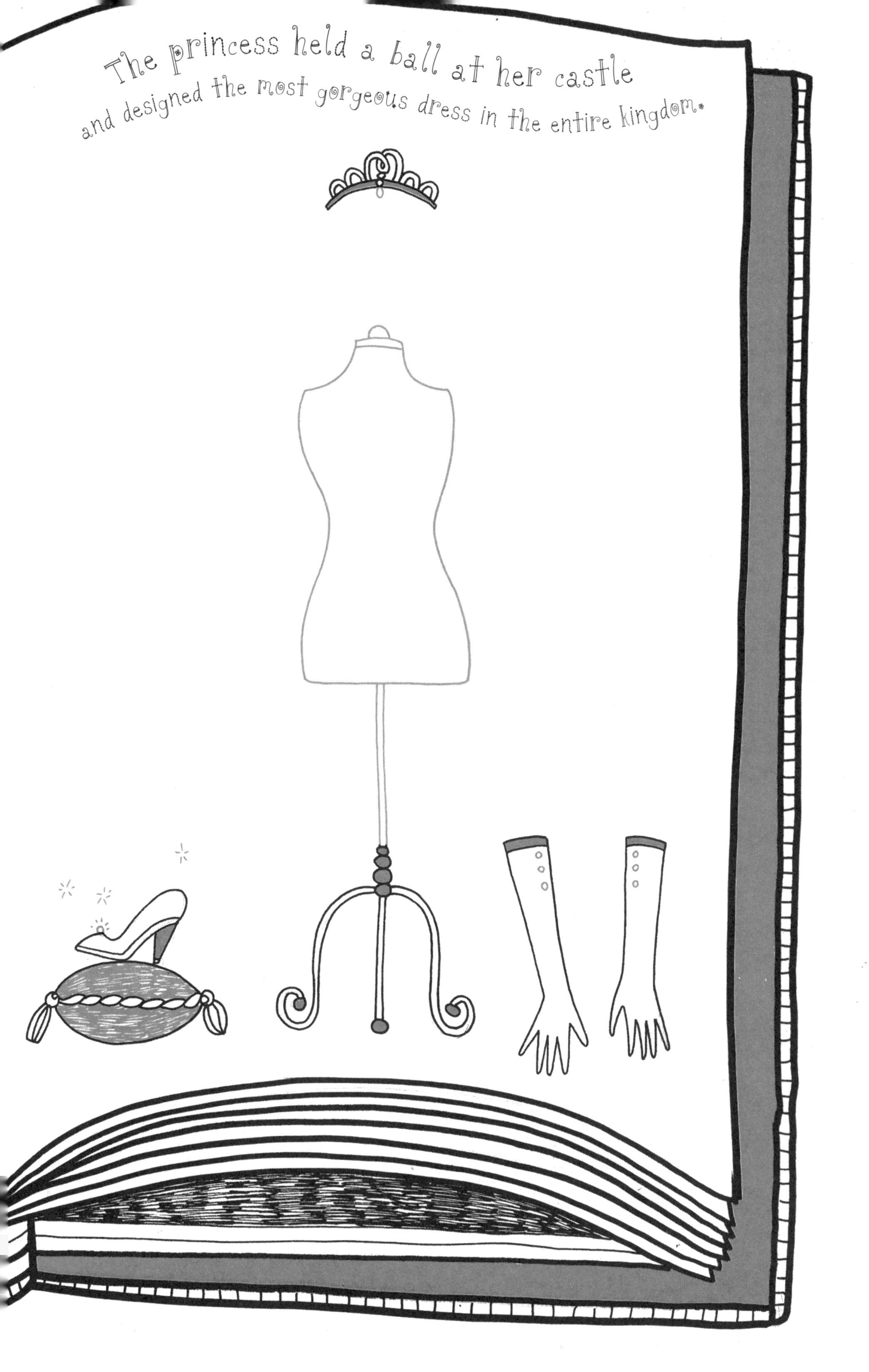
The princess held a ball at her castle
and designed the most gorgeous dress in the entire kingdom.

DOODLE
SOME SPARKLY
GEMS AND
JEWELRY
DIAMONDS ARE A GIRL'S BEST FRIEND!

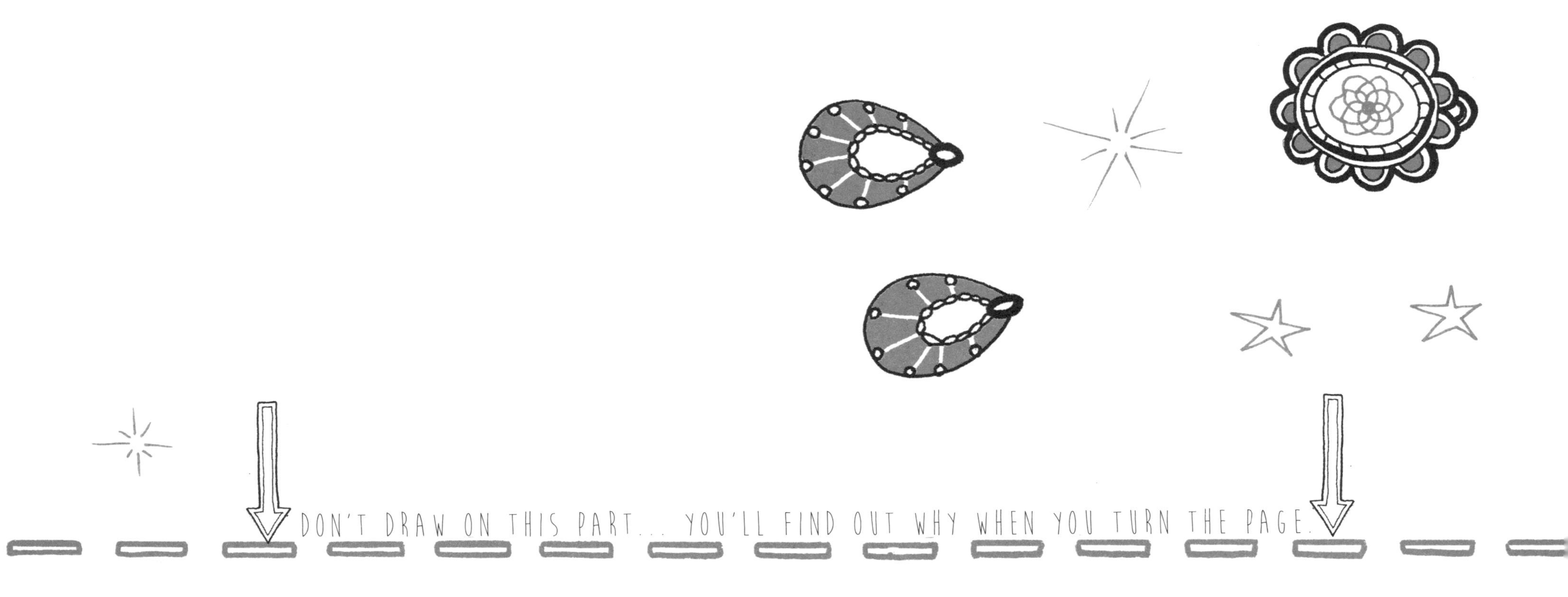
DON'T DRAW ON THIS PART... YOU'LL FIND OUT WHY WHEN YOU TURN THE PAGE.

Dress to impress and
doodle yourself a
designer closet.

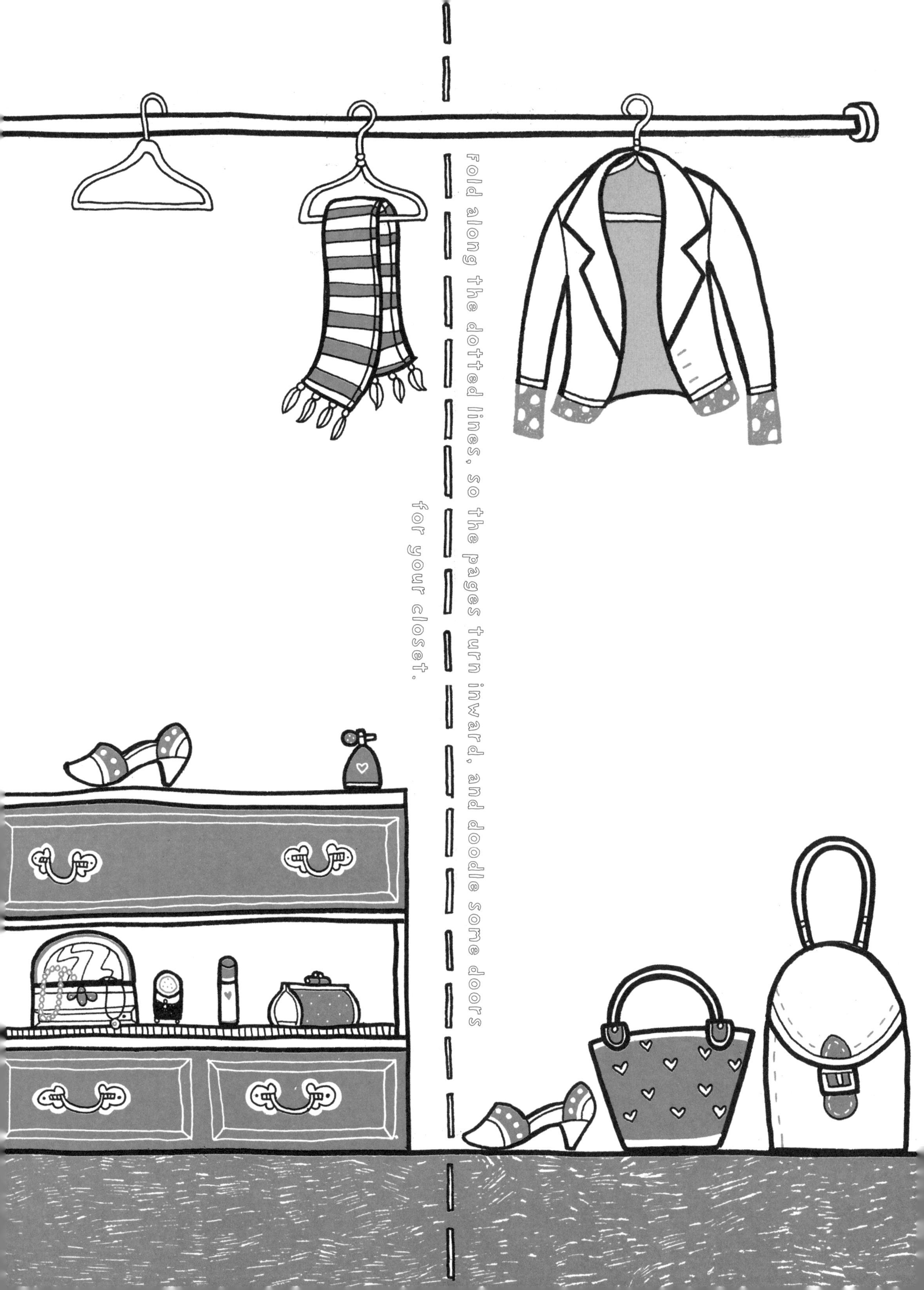
fold along the dotted lines, so the pages turn inward, and doodle some doors for your closet.

KNOCK KNOCK!
Who's there?

Draw yourself in here!

Cook up some delicious doodles for the cake shop.

Light up
the sky with
fireworks and
BIG BANGS!

close your eyes, listen
to some music, and
doodle whatever comes
into your head.

You'll need to turn the page around for this one...

Pick your top five tunes and design some amazing album covers for them.

UP, UP, AND AWAY!

DOODLE IN A TEENY TINY TOWN BELOW...

TRACE AROUND YOUR HANDS AND CREATE SOME STYLISH NAIL DESIGNS TO GIVE THEM

THE WOW FACTOR!

Time to turn the book around again! Doodle some funny faces in the circles below...

...you'll find out why later!

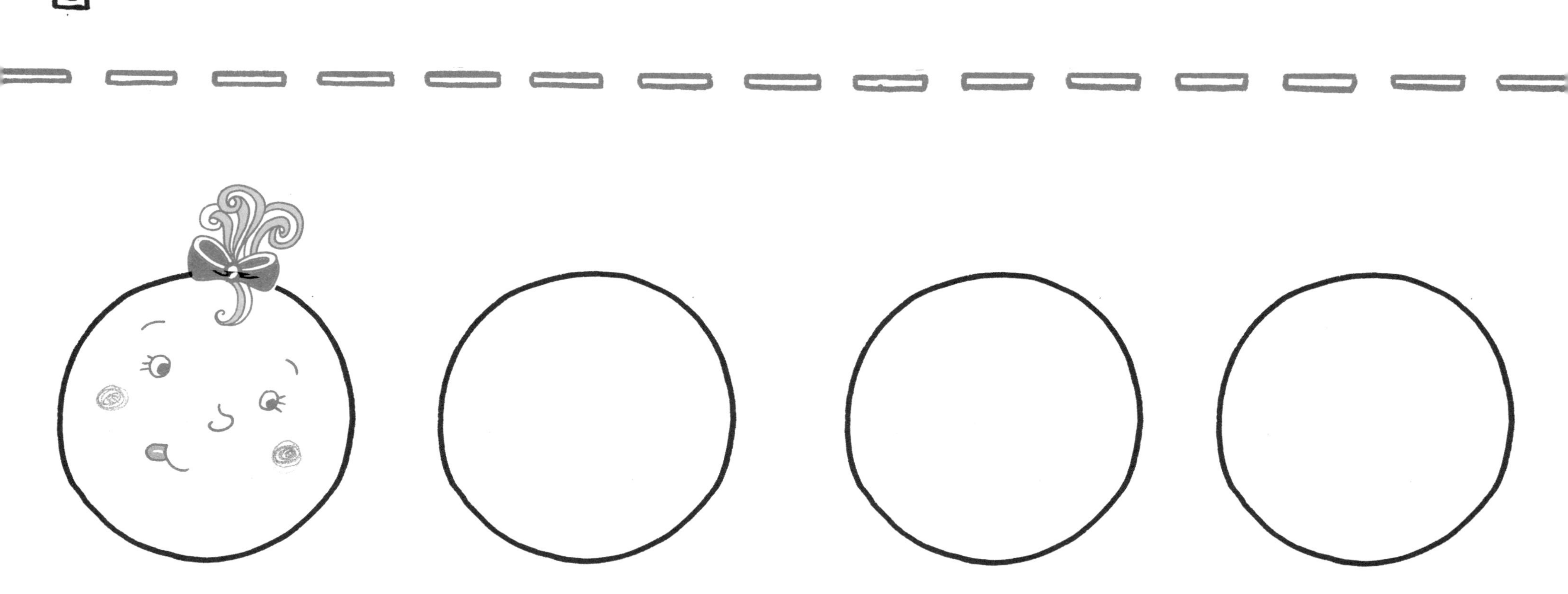

Go crazy on these blank pages—draw with every pen you own!

NEXT... Fold the page in on itself along this black dotted line.

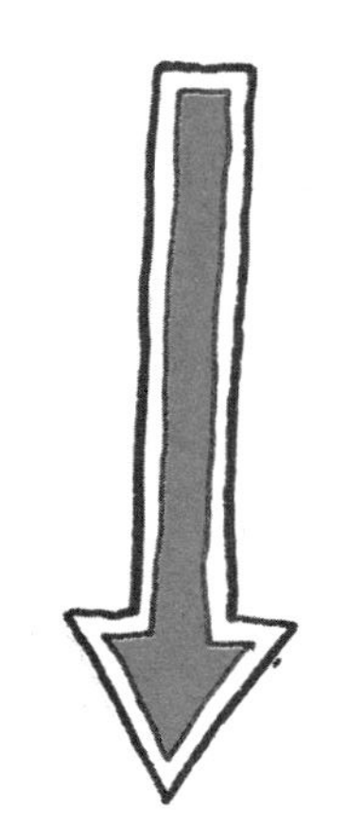

**THEN...** Fold this page in on itself along this pink dotted line, and doodle some bodies in the squares that appear.

Use this space to draw...

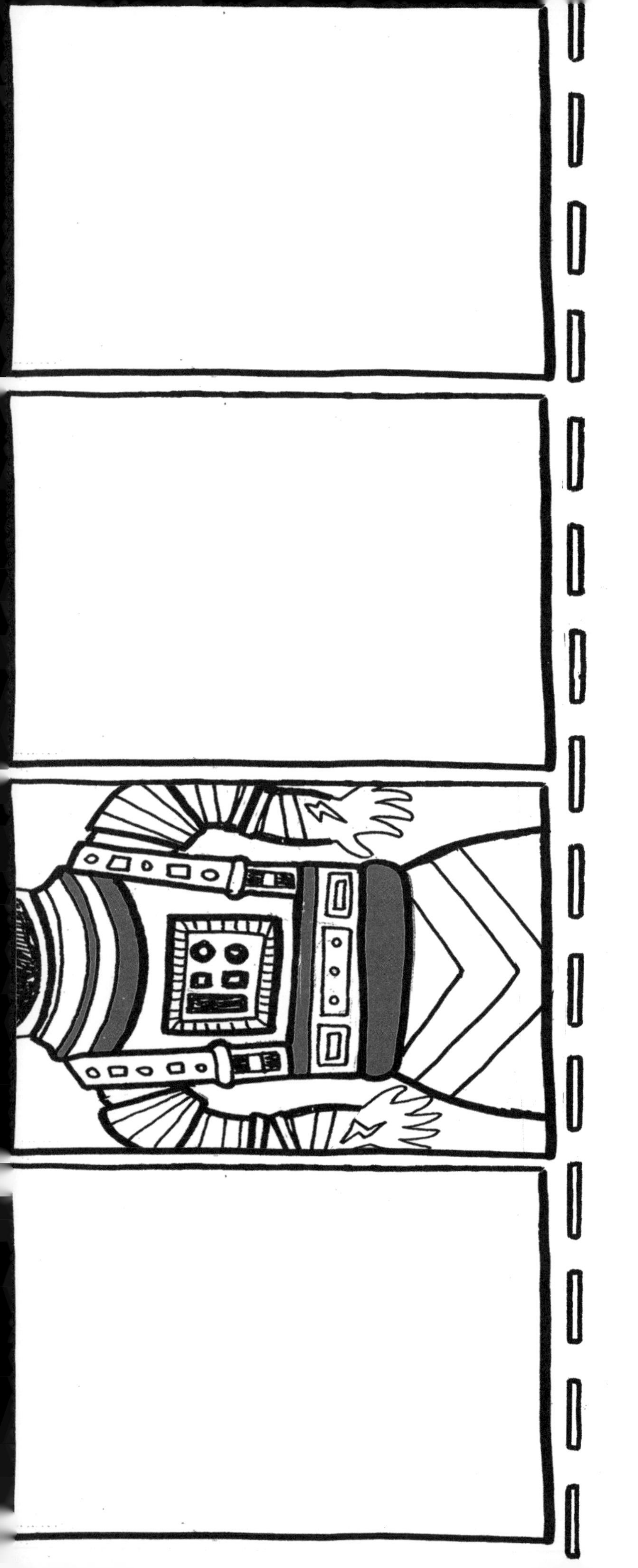

...what you will look like in 50 years!

Now draw in some funny legs!

Hubble bubble...
...doodle some witches flying
on broomsticks!

Turn these wiggly lines into spooky ghosts...
...what else gives you goosebumps?

TURN ON THE TV. WHAT DO YOU SEE? DOODLE IT!

All aboard! who's on the bus?

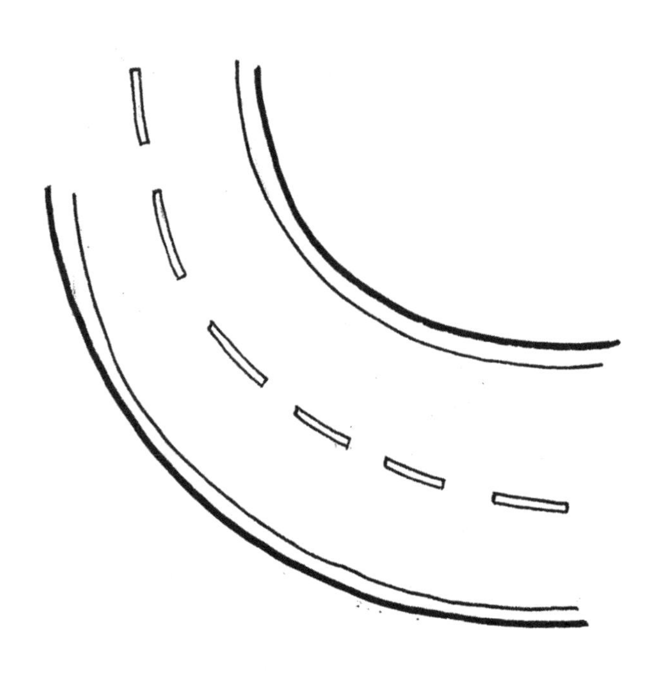

And where are they going?

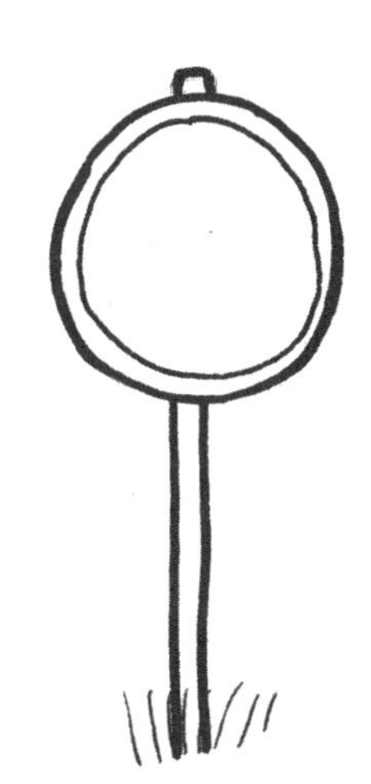

What did you dream
about last night?

How are you feeling today?

What makes you smile?

haha!!

What's on your mind?

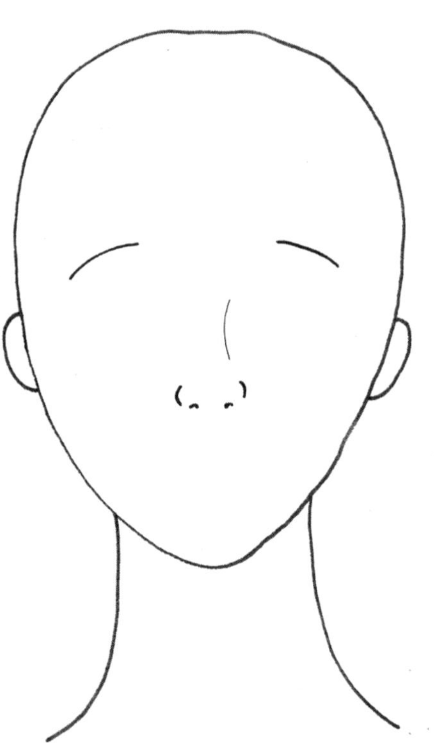

Fill in the name of a movie you'd love to star in.
Doodle yourself on the red carpet!

1. Take one thumbprint...

2. Add some wiggly and straight lines...

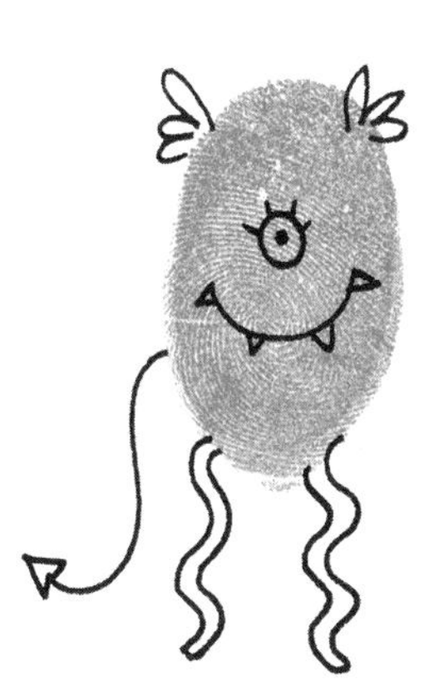

3. Create lots of cute doodles all over the page!

What does the future hold for you?

DOODLE SOME PRETTY PATTERNS ON THIS FAN.
NOW CUT OUT THE FAN AND FOLD BACK AND FORTH ALONG THE DOTTED LINES TO MAKE YOUR OWN 3-D DOODLES!
TURN THE PAGE TO FIND OUT WHAT TO DO WITH THESE PINK STRIPS...

YOU CAN DECORATE THE BACK OF YOUR FAN AS WELL.

COPY THIS PIGGY DOODLE NEXT TO EACH STRIP.

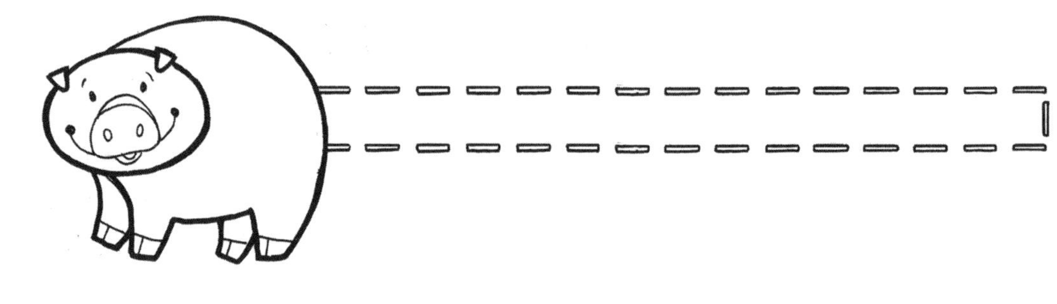

SNIP ALONG THE DOTTED LINES AND WRAP EACH STRIP TIGHTLY AROUND YOUR PENCIL TO CREATE CURLY TAILS FOR YOUR PIGGIES!

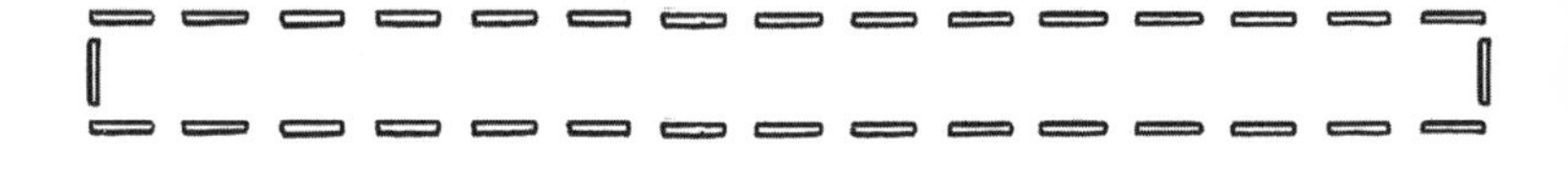

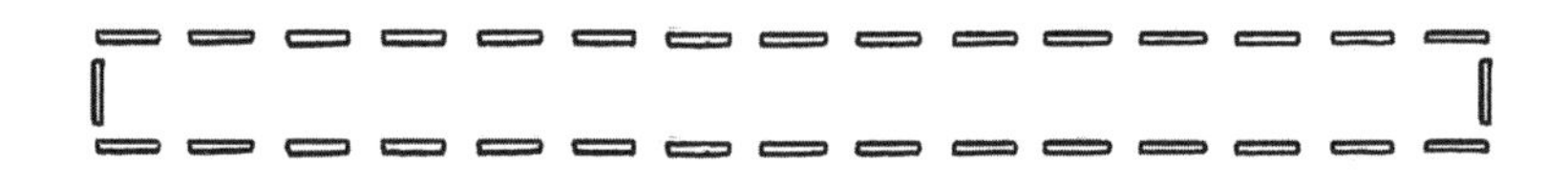

Place a coin under the paper and rub over it with the side of a crayon.
Keep going until your piggy bank is full!

Got any bright ideas...
doodle your best ones in the bulbs!

Where would you go...

...dressed like this?

What beauty products...

...have you always wanted?

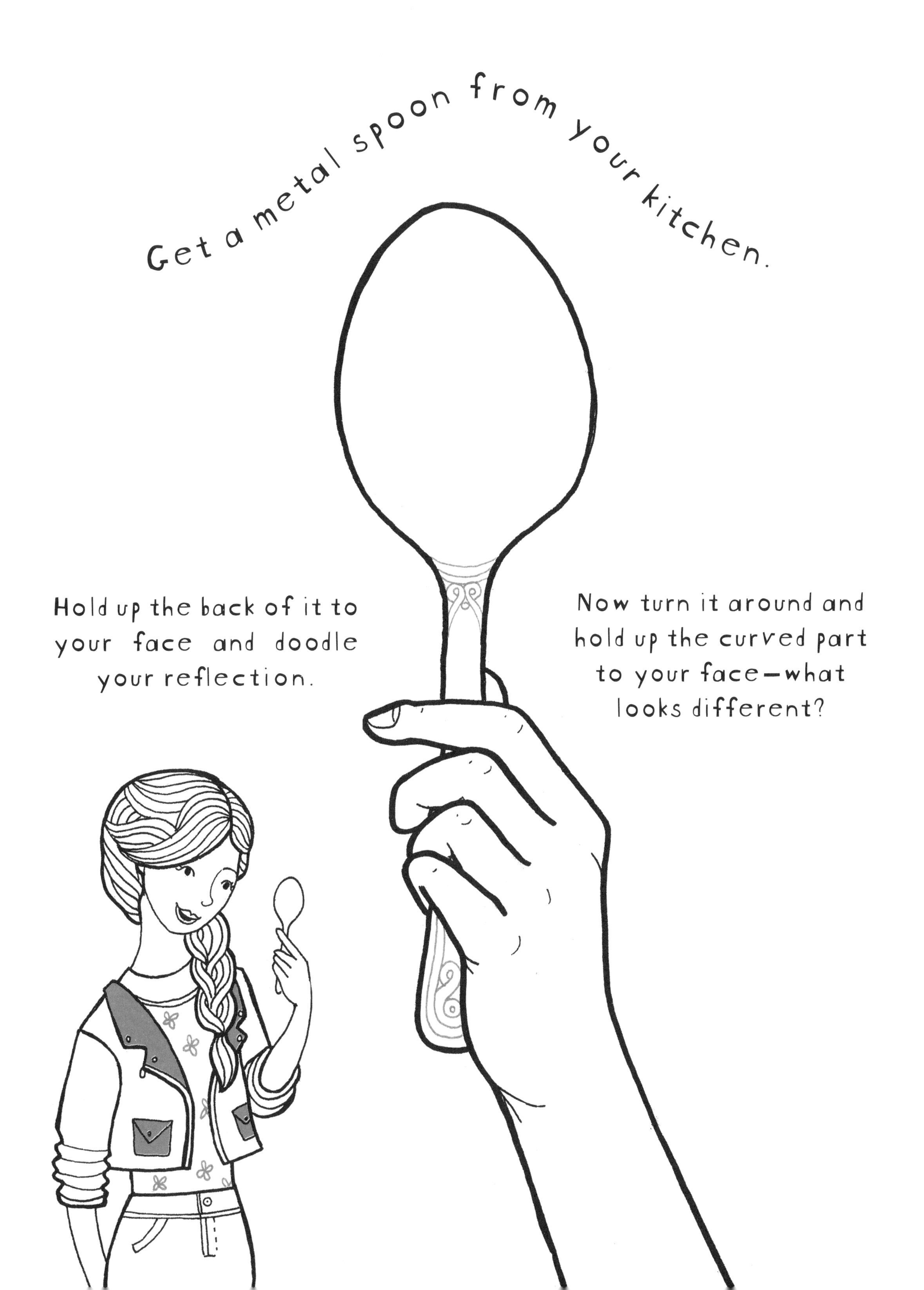
Get a metal spoon from your kitchen.
Hold up the back of it to your face and doodle your reflection.
Now turn it around and hold up the curved part to your face—what looks different?

Bad hair day? Turn these lovely locks into some crazy doodles.

Fill this winter wonderland with twirling, swirling ice-skaters.

Doodle your favorite three things about winter in these snow globes.

It's easy to doodle...
...a penguin!

ADD SOME DOODLES TO THESE SNOWFLAKES, SO NO TWO ARE THE SAME.

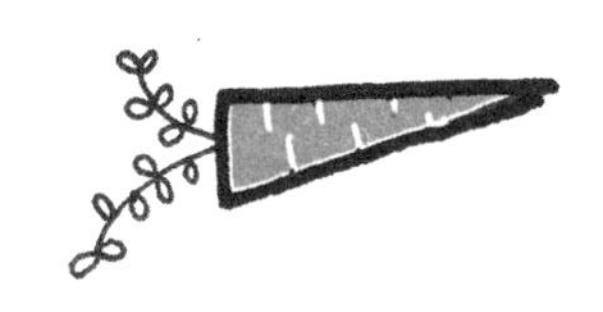

How many snowmen can you draw in 60 seconds?
Your time starts...
NOW!

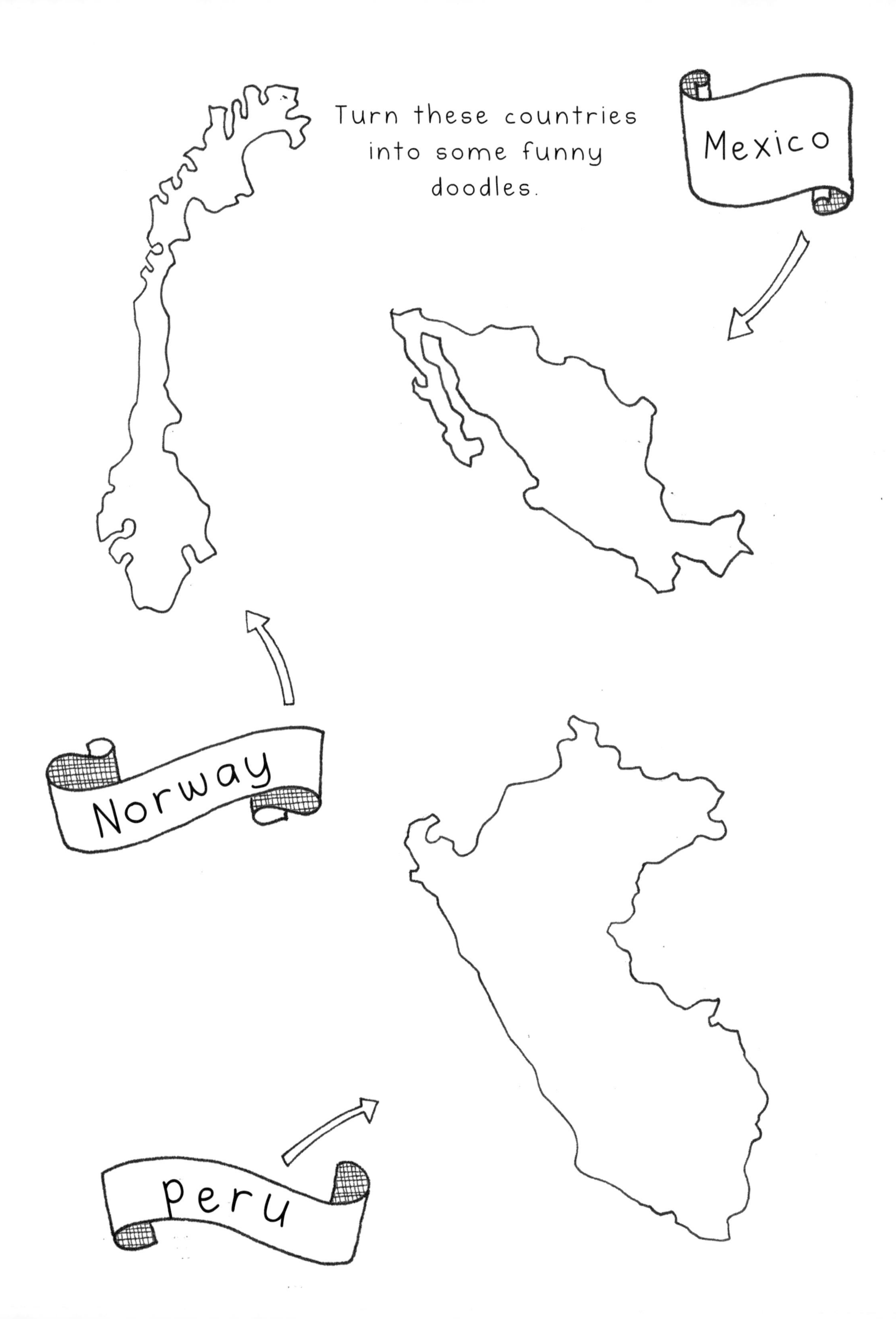
Turn these countries into some funny doodles.
Mexico
Norway
peru

Add some doodles to this

map of the world!

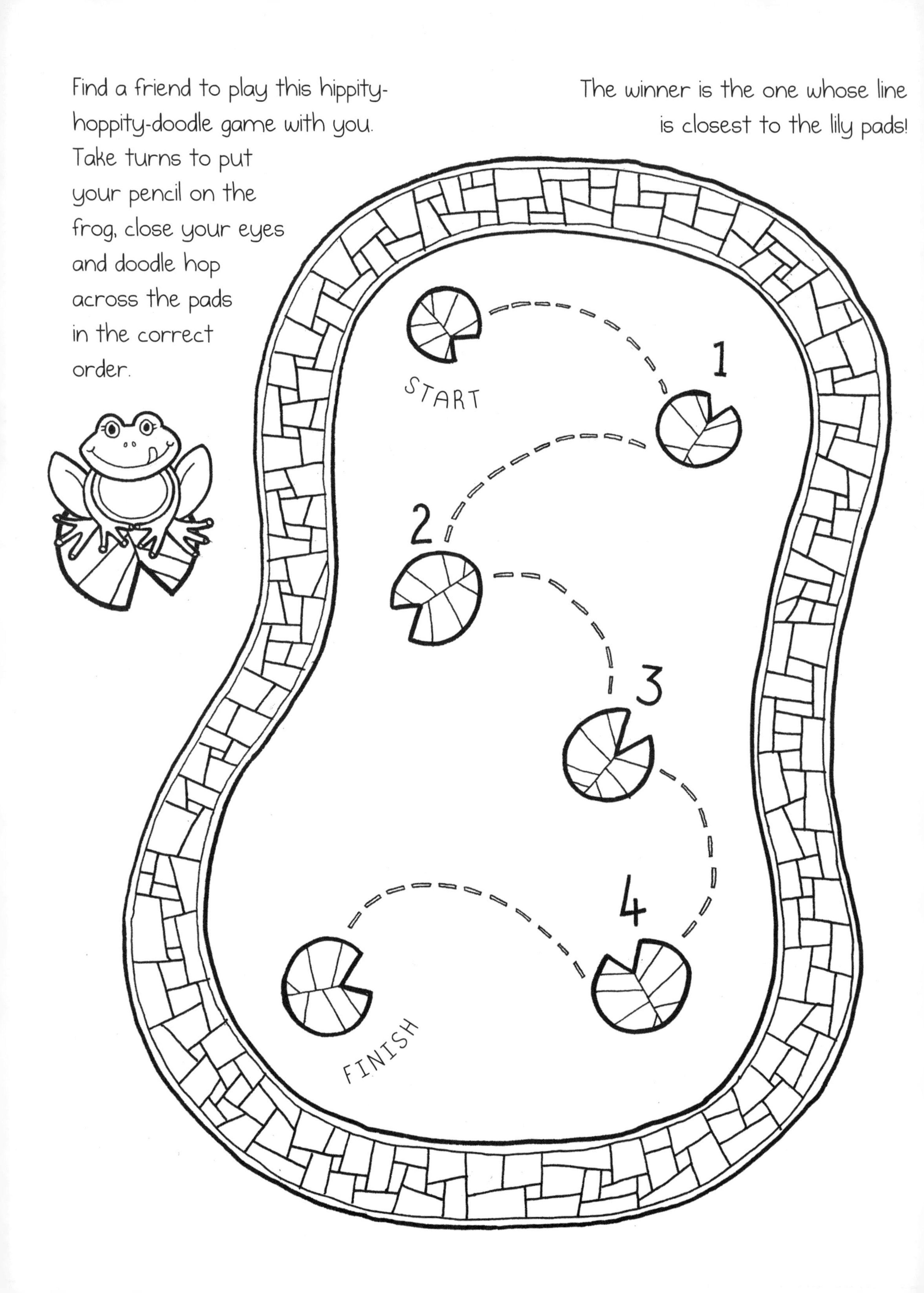
Find a friend to play this hippity-hoppity-doodle game with you. Take turns to put your pencil on the frog, close your eyes and doodle hop across the pads in the correct order.
The winner is the one whose line is closest to the lily pads!
START
1
2
3
4
FINISH

What a catch!
Doodle something funny on the end of the fishing line.

what did you have to

DOODLE IN A BIKE FOR THIS GIRL TO RIDE.

WHERE WILL IT TAKE HER?

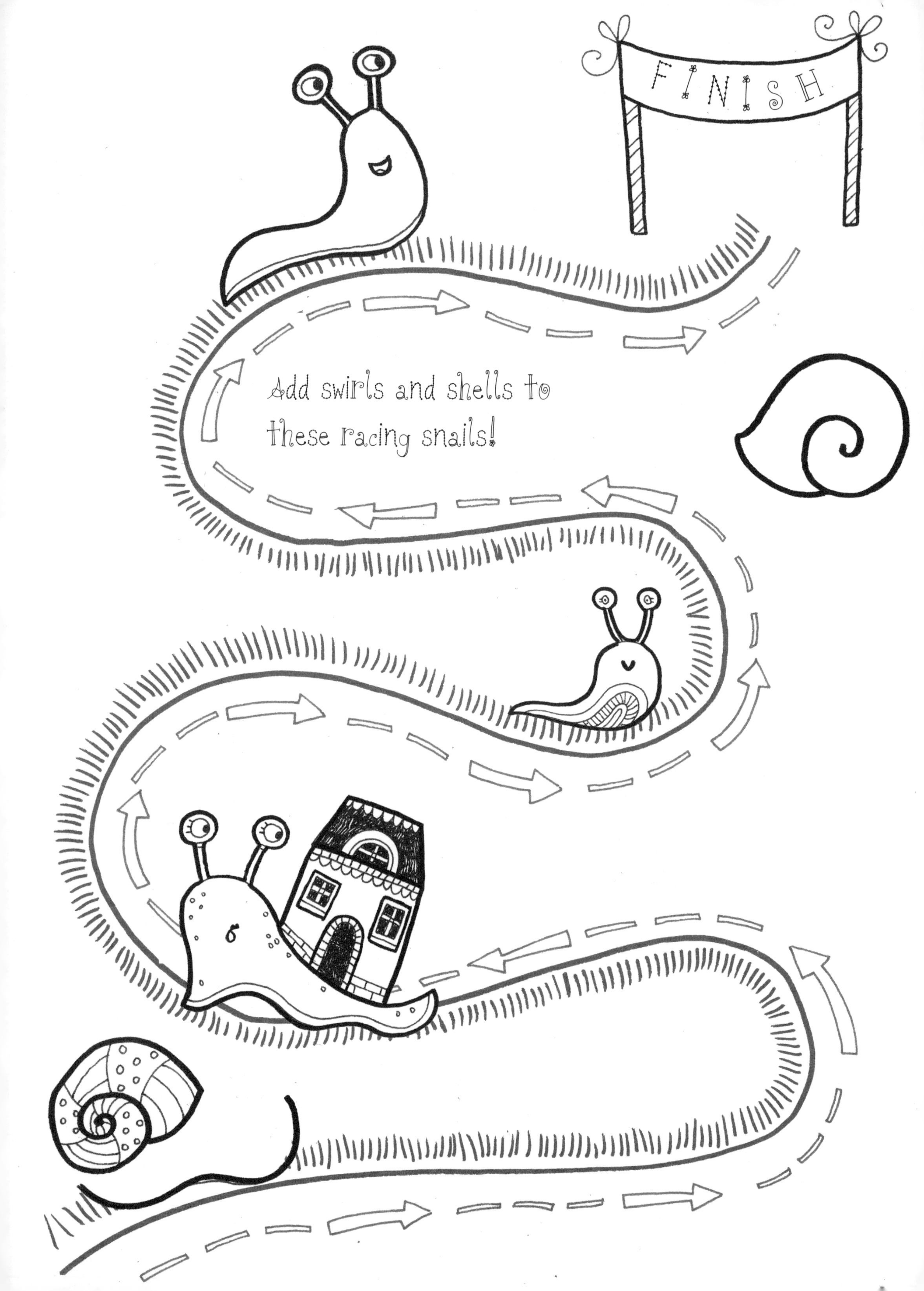
FINISH
Add swirls and shells to
these racing snails!

1. 2. 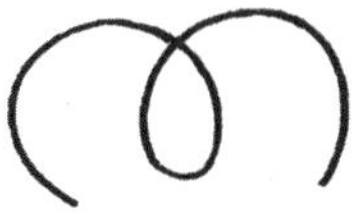 3.  4.

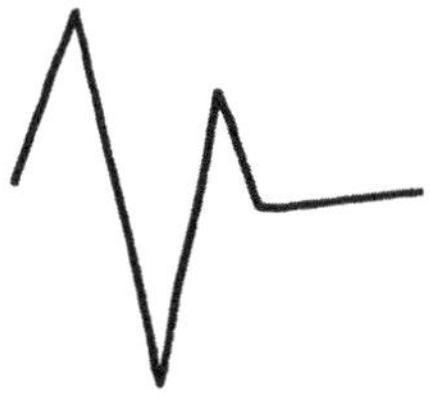

5.  6.  7.  8.

9. 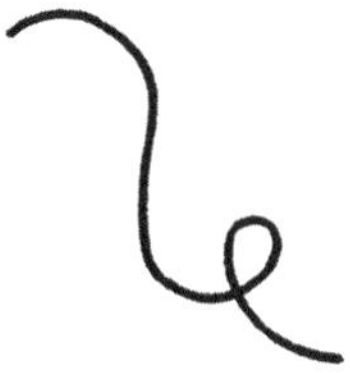 10.

Time yourself to see how quickly you can turn these ten squiggles into drawings:

__ mins and __ seconds

Now draw ten more and see if your friend can beat your time!

1. 2. 3. 4.

5. 6. 7. 8.

9. 10.

# CREATE A MASTERPIECE...

...OR DOODLE A FUNNY PICTURE INSTEAD

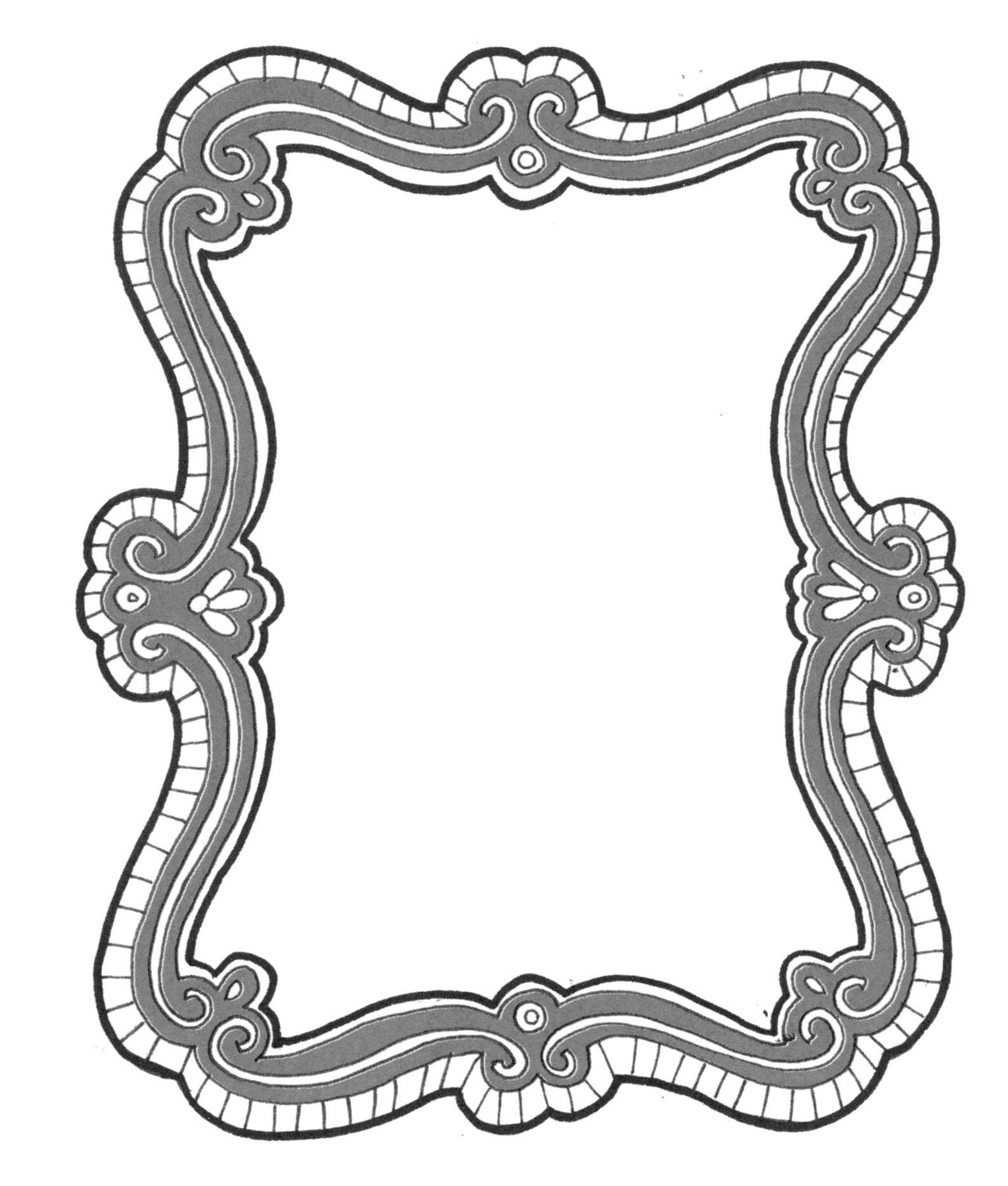

Dream up a different doodle to fill every circle on the page...